ANSWERS TO

FIRST
AID IN
SPELLING

Jan Gallow &
Karen Morrison

HODDER
EDUCATION
AN HACHETTE UK COMPANY

Every effort has been made to trace all copyright holders, but if any have been
inadvertently overlooked the Publishers will be pleased to make the necessary
arrangements at the first opportunity.

Hachette UK's policy is to use papers that are natural, renewable and recyclable
products and made from wood grown in sustainable forests. The logging and
manufacturing processes are expected to conform to the environmental regulations
of the country of origin.

Orders: please contact Bookpoint Ltd, 130 Milton Park, Abingdon, Oxon OX14 4SB.
Telephone: (44) 01235 827720. Fax: (44) 01235 400454. Lines are open 9.00–5.00,
Monday to Saturday, with a 24-hour message answering service. Visit our website at
www.hoddereducation.com.

© Jan Gallow & Karen Morrison, 2013
First published in 2013 by
Hodder Education,
An Hachette UK Company
Carmelite House, 50 Victoria Embankment,
London EC4Y 0DZ

Impression number 5 4 3 2
Year 2017 2016 2015

Typeset in ITC Garamond Book 11/14 points by Datapage (India) Pvt. Ltd.
Printed in Great Britain by CPI Group (UK) Ltd, Croydon, CR0 4YY

A catalogue record for this title is available from the British Library.

ISBN: 978 1444 186444

Contents

Note: For those questions where various answers are possible, check that the answers are spelt correctly.

English spelling

Exercise 1 Page 1

1. sure
2. losing
3. height
4. therefore
5. foreign
6. believe

Exercise 2 Page 3

a. cal(l)ed   ex(c)eed   judg(e)ment   re(a)lly
bound(a)ry   gran(d)dad   jumpe(d)   sc(h)ool
definit(e)ly   humor(o)us   nar(r)ator   stoppe(d)
diff(e)rent   im(m)ediate   notic(e)able   sud(d)enly
embarras(s)   int(e)resting   pe(o)ple   w(h)en

b. Oral exercise

Exercise 3 Page 3

a. See **b.** for syllables to clap.

b. ac • com • mo • date   chil • dren   go • ing   pos • ses • sion
an • i • mal   en • vi • ron • ment   lit • tle   prac • ti • cal
an • oth • er   ex • pla • na • tion   look • ing   some • thing
be • gan   gar • den   oc • ca • sion   win • dow
busi • ness   gi • ant   op • por • tu • ni • ty   writ • ten

c. Oral exercise

Exercise 4 Page 5

a. Method explained in question book on pages 3-4.

b. Method explained in question book on pages 4-5.

Exercise 5 Page 6

a. <u>believe</u> – There is a **lie** in me.
<u>separate</u> – People smell **a rat** in me.
<u>desert</u> – I am **s**andy with one **s**.
<u>dessert</u> – Another name for me is **sweets** with 2 **s**'s.
<u>eight</u> – I have a fatty and a thinny and a **g h t**.
<u>piece</u> – I am a part of the **pie**.
<u>gauge</u> – **a** and **u** stay in alphabetical order when you spell me.

b. Keep great out of <u>grateful</u>.
Really **h**ope **ye** <u>rhymes</u> with **me**.
Rhythm has your **t**wo **h**ips **m**oving.
Always **add** me to your <u>address.</u>
A <u>friend</u> is with you until the **end**.

c. hear / here
stationery / stationary
loose / lose

d. Various answers are possible, for example:
ne**cess**ary: Never eat cod – eat **s**moked **s**almon and remain young.
February: In London, it is **brr** in Feb**r**uary.
their: The **heir** will inherit **their** money.
there: It's not **here** it's **there**.

Exercise 6 Page 7

Method explained in question book on page 7.

Exercise 7 Page 8

Method explained in question book on pages 7–8.

Exercise 8 Page 9

a. Oral exercise

b. Various other answers are possible in addition to the following:

<u>am</u> <u>bition</u>	<u>fortun<u>ate</u></u>	p<u>aper</u>	trans<u>port</u> <u>ation</u>
b<u>ear</u>	gr<u>eat</u>	pro<u>nunciation</u>	w<u>ate</u>r
<u>began</u>	i<u>l</u>legal	psy<u>chic</u>	w<u>ant</u>
c<u>our</u> <u>age</u>	<u>in</u>st<u>ead</u>	<u>re</u>staur<u>ant</u>	wh<u>en</u>
d<u>anger</u>ous	ki<u>lo</u>gram	sh<u>out</u>ed	wh<u>ere</u>
de<u>livery</u>	l<u>anguage</u>	stu<u>dent</u>	wh<u>ite</u>
<u>drag</u> <u>on</u>	me<u>ta</u>phor	<u>things</u>	y<u>ear</u>

c. Any memory tricks for three words from the list that students find helpful, for example:

stu**dent**: A stu**dent** made a **dent** in my bicycle.

sh**out**ed: The teacher sent me **out** of the classroom because I sh**out**ed **out** the answer.

things: Healthy **thin**gs keep me **thin**.

Exercise 9 Page 10

Method explained in question book on pages 9–10.

Exercise 10 Page 12

a. Personal response
b. Method explained in question book on page 11.
c. Personal response
d. Methods explained in question book on pages 2–10.

Phonetic rules

Exercise 1 Page 13

a. Three words from each of the following lists:
    short a sound: apple, bat, can, hat, lap, mat, pan, van
    short e sound: egg, bell, elephant, except
    short i sound: ink, pill, pin, thin, win
    short o sound: pot, not, log, orange
    short u sound: bun, bug, much, mum, plum, tub, umbrella

b. Any three additional words for each of the five short vowel sounds, for example:
    short a sound: cat, fat, stand
    short e sound: fell, sell, smell
    short i sound: bin, tin, swim
    short o sound: hot, lots, clot
    short u sound: fun, run, strum

Exercise 2 Page 15

ape	funny	odd	these
bake	got	pen	type
cap	hope	pin	tyre
cape	hop	pine	use
cake	ice	price	up
complete	lane	run	vine
dam	let	rent	wet
dame	mat	rice	white
end	melt	rise	winter
every	mite	site	yes
fire	nun	sit	zebra
fore	nose	spy	
for	ore	tale	

4

Exercise 3 Pages 17–18

a. Five words from each of the following lists:
ai: aid, air, bail, chain, chair, dairy, fail, fairy, gain, hail, mail, main, nail, pail, pair, plain, rain, sail, tail, train, wait
ay: clay, crayon, day, decay, hay, play, ray, say, stay, tray, way
a with a silent e: ate, ape, bane, cake, came, cane, care, dame, dare, face, fate, game, gate, glare, grade, hate, lake, lane, made, make, name, plane, rake, save, take, whale

b. fair, slay, rain, air, say, tray, wait, hair, play

c. fly, crystal, oxygen, flair, hymn, him, playground, mystery, while, pride

d.
1. br<u>a</u>ve – fearless
2. ch<u>oo</u>se – pick one
3. d<u>ea</u>r – precious
4. p<u>a</u>le – light in colour
5. r<u>i</u>ce – starchy food
6. t<u>ea</u>ch – show how to
7. h<u>u</u>ge – very big
8. r<u>ea</u>l – genuine
9. cl<u>ea</u>n – not dirty

e. Any ten words for each vowel combination: ee, ea, ie, ai, for example:

ee	ea	ie	ai
beech	beach	belief	abstain
discreet	bead	brief	Claire
esteem	beak	carried	drain
feeble	bear	Debbie	grain
feed	beat	diesel	liaise
indeed	earring	diet	obtain
keep	fear	field	praise
speed	team	fiend	quaint
week	tease	grief	retain
wheeze	weary	pierce	taint

Exercise 4 Page 19

a. It is not my <u>fault</u>.
My brother likes to <u>draw</u> pictures.
It is against the <u>law</u> to steal.
<u>Autumn</u> is my favourite season.
My little sister is very <u>naughty</u>.
I like school <u>because</u> I learn a lot.

b. August, awful, laundry, saucer, haunted, applause, thoughtful, dinosaur

5

Exercise 5 Pages 20–21

a. owl
towel
tower
cloud
count
mountain
noun
sound
allow

b.

A	J	P	O	U	N	D	G	C
B	T	O	O	C	U	A	H	L
C	O	W	A	R	D	B	F	O
D	W	E	P	O	V	C	O	W
E	E	R	O	W	W	D	U	N
F	L	O	U	D	X	D	N	M
G	L	M	Q	S	Y	E	D	K
H	O	W	E	V	E	R	I	L
I	K	N	R	T	Z	F	J	P

Exercise 6 Pages 21–22

a. carbon, harbour, hard, cart, mark, market, pardon, part, dark, garden, lard, partner, party

b. tar
garden
harbour
cart
car
hard
dark

c. Any sentences that show the meaning of bargain, market, pardon, remark heart, for example:

The shirt was a bargain in the sale.

My mother sent me to the market to buy oranges, apples, pears and bananas.

"Pardon?" he said, when he didn't hear the speaker.

"That remark was uncalled for," scolded the teacher.

His heart pounded when he was scared.

Exercise 7 Page 23

bird, after, thirst, boxer, circle, hammer, search, hear, girl, kerb, mermaid, mother, dirty, river, early, tiger, water, earth

Exercise 8 Page 23

a. quarter, corn, form, correct, cord, normal, orange, sorry, report, short, war, warrior

b. acorn, forbid, glory, organ, pore, borrow, porridge, tornado, tomorrow, reward, warm, quarrel

Exercise 9 Page 25

a. friend, eighteen, siege, vein, field, reign, cashier, receipt, relief, deceit, fierce, veil

b. It is better to give than to <u>receive</u>.

What you <u>believe</u> you will achieve.

Love your <u>friends</u> and <u>neighbours</u> like yourself.

<u>Neither</u> a borrower nor a lender be.

All things grow with time, except <u>grief</u>.

<u>Experience</u> is the mother of wisdom.

<u>Variety</u> is the spice of life.

c.
1. believe
2. achieve
3. receive
4. either
5. seize
6. forfeit
7. friend
8. science
9. niece

d. Any sentences that show the meaning of friend, fiend, piece, peace, for example:

I'm going to the cinema with my best friend.

Superman fought the evil fiend.

He ate a large piece of cake on his birthday.

After the war there was peace.

Exercise 10 Page 27

a. cat, king, bake, cake, make, came, cane, claim, kettle, key, kingfisher, crayon, cute

b. back
   cute
   kettle
   luck
   rock

c. catch, cane, tick, kitten, suck, clock, quack, crime, cucumber, camel, kiss, king

Exercise 11 Page 28

a. Oral exercise

b. Personal response

c. Methods explained in question book on pages 2–10.

Exercise 12 Pages 28–29

a.
cinema	cancel	pace	price
celery	centre	mice	rice
cider	carpet	peace	science
corn	certain	ocean	trace
cucumber	face	cute	twice
camel	dance	logic	voice
brace	decent	cabbage	college
ace	notice	cry	

b. The following words have a g sound:
agent	large	garden	grin
germ	rag	gum	gold
legend	gutter	gull	original
age	going	gem	
gentle	giraffe	grim	
ginger	good	girl	

The following words have both a c and a g sound:
logic	cabbage	college

c.

Hard c sound (like a k)	Soft c sound (like an s)	Hard g sound (like a g)	Soft g sound (like a j)
cabbage	ace	garden	age
camel	brace	girl	agent
cancel	cancel	going	cabbage
carpet	celery	gold	college
college	centre	good	gem
corn	certain	grim	gentle
cry	cider	grin	germ
cucumber	cinema	gull	ginger
cute	dance	gum	giraffe
logic	decent	gutter	large
	face	rag	legend
	mice		logic
	notice		original
	ocean		
	pace		
	peace		
	price		
	rice		
	science		
	trace		
	twice		
	voice		

d. Method explained in question book on pages 3-5.

Exercise 13 Pages 29–30

a. dodge   badge   smudge
   nudge   edge   judge
            ridge

b. gem, glue, jump, jacket, juice, glum

Exercise 14 **Pages 30–31**

a. chilly   match   chin   watch

chilly	match	chin	watch
teacher	chew	hatch	branch
pitch	search	chair	change
champion	watch	chimpanzee	cheese
church	beach	chip	cheetah
chain	kitchen	march	chase
catch	channel	chalk	chatter
cheat	check	child	cheap

b. teacher
cheetah
chalk
watch
child
beach
chair
chew

c. Animals: cheetah, chimpanzee and any three others
Types of food: chip, cheese and any three others

Exercise 15 **Page 33**

a. fuse, because, cheese, lose, seize, choose, snooze, ooze, freeze, noise, please

b. bussing, hizzing, (fizzy), (missing), kizzing, mizz, acrozz, (class), pissa, pussle, exprezz, bzss, (passing), mazzive, carelezz, (across), drzz, blissard, (message)

c. buzzing, hissing, kissing, miss, across, pizza, puzzle, express, buzz, massive, careless, dress, blizzard

d. scene, fascinate, muscle, science, scissors

e. Various answers are possible, for example:

Excuse me, could you <u>assist</u> me?

I can't see so well, so I have to wear <u>glasses</u>.

The pupils in my <u>class</u> are all good at spelling.

I didn't know the answer so I had to <u>guess</u>.

I couldn't answer the phone, so he left a <u>message</u>.

<u>Press</u> this button to open the door.

I like to go camping in the <u>wilderness</u>.

Exercise 16 Page 35

a. Any sets of three words with one, two or more syllables that start with the given letters, for example:

Starts with	One syllable	Two syllables	More than two syllables
fa	far farm fat	farmer father fatter	fabulous faculty fashionable
fe	feat feed feel	feeble feeder fellow	feasible fearlessly February
fi	fit fight file	fighting filing finance	fictional fictitious finalise
fo	foe foam folk	focus foggy folder	foliage focusing forgiving
fu	fun fudge fluff	funny funnel fluffy	funnier fundamental fluffier
fl	flow flag flask	flowing flavour flannel	flamingo flexible flowering
fr	fright frame frost	fragile framing frosty	fragility frangipani frostily

b. dwarfs, safe, coffee, refer, beefy, fizzled, cough, enough, elephant, fluffy, sniffed, stuff, suffer, difference, buffalo, effective, coffin, from, theft, graph

11

c. cough, rough, elephant, physical, tough, phantom, telephone, laughter, trophy, draught, phrase, nephew, atmosphere, orphan, prophet, geography, enough, dolphin

d. Methods explained in question book on pages 2–10.

Exercise 17 Page 36

a.
1. stopped	9. fluffy
2. dropped	10. buzzing
3. running	11. hissing
4. hidden	12. pulling
5. shining	13. growing
6. beginning	14. loving
7. spinning	15. lacking
8. falling	

b. Personal response

c. Methods explained in question book on pages 2–10.

Exercise 18 Pages 36–37

a.
1. wash
2. wander
3. wand
4. watch
5. child
6. wound

b.
1. seat	8. claw
2. holiday	9. saucer
3. window	10. loud
4. threw	11. food
5. push	12. enjoyed
6. paint	13. curly
7. point	14. clear

c. cl(aw)

cl(ear)

c(ur)ly

(e)nj(oy)ed

f(oo)d

h(o)l(i)d(a)y

l(ou)d

p(ai)nt

p(oi)nt

p(u)sh

s(au)cer

s(ea)t

thr(ew)

w(i)nd(o)w

d. Any sets of five words with the given sounds and spellings, for example:

c as in cat: class, coffee, commit, cone, cough

eh as in bread: breath, head, instead, ready, steady

ur as in fur: burden, burgle, burn, church, further

ee as in ear: beach, bead, leaf, meat, reach

c as in cell: ceiling, circle, civilise, emancipation, lice

s as in sugar: issue, pressure, reassure, sure, tissue

f as in fair: flower, forget, grateful, huff, life

f as in laugh: cough, enough, rough, tough, trough

tt as in cattle: battle, better, bottle, kitty, little

z as in fuse: apologise, exercise, raise, rise, rose

Structural rules

Exercise 1 Page 39

a. & b.

Singular	Plural	Singular	Plural
bedroom	bedrooms	horse	horses
bicycle	bicycles	house	houses
book	books	key	keys
boy	boys	king	kings
broom	brooms	kitchen	kitchens
car	cars	mother	mothers
dog	dogs	paper	papers
door	doors	place	places
dragon	dragons	plant	plants
duck	ducks	rabbit	rabbits
eye	eyes	school	schools
father	fathers	stick	sticks
friend	friends	town	towns
garden	gardens	train	trains
girl	girls	tree	trees
head	heads	window	windows

c. Any sentences containing the correct plurals of the given words, for example:
  1. The girls saw the cows and bulls on the farms.
  2. The boys watched the mechanics fixing the cars at the garages.
  3. The parents took the girls presents when they visited them in the hospitals.
  4. The children climbed the trees when the parents were away from the homes.
  5. Zoos keep their monkeys in cages.

d. The crazy <u>apes</u> threw <u>sticks</u> and <u>stones</u> at the <u>onlookers</u>.
   The pretty <u>tins</u> were decorated with colourful <u>buttons</u> and silver <u>beads</u>.
   The energetic <u>boys</u> jumped across the <u>streams</u>.
   The rowdy <u>girls</u> cheered and danced to encourage the <u>athletes</u>.
   The <u>winners</u> of the <u>races</u> received gold <u>medals</u>.

Exercise 2 Pages 40–41

a. one church, many churches   one sandwich, many sandwiches
one circus, many circuses   one hutch, many hutches
one lioness, many lionesses   one waltz, many waltzes
one match, many matches   one wish, many wishes
one glass, many glasses   one gas, many gases

b.

		3. d	4. b	5. d	6. b
	2. f	i	u	r	u
1. b	o	s	s	e	s
o	x	h	h	s	e
x	e	e	e	s	s
e	s	s	s	e	
s				s	

c. Any sentences containing the correct plurals of the given words, for example:
  1. The fairy godmothers waved their magic wands and the princesses appeared in the castles.
  2. Some frogs' skins have red patches.
  3. The bosses told the workers to put their belongings in boxes.
  4. The cars passed beautiful trees as they sped down the freeways.
  5. The witnesses spoke to the reporters about the accidents.

Exercise 3 Pages 41–42

a.

Nouns ending in a vowel + y		Nouns ending in a consonant + y	
Singular	**Plural**	**Singular**	**Plural**
key	keys	puppy	puppies
alley	alleys	assembly	assemblies
day	days	baby	babies
donkey	donkeys	country	countries
holiday	holidays	energy	energies
journey	journeys	fly	flies
monkey	monkeys	industry	industries
play	plays	lady	ladies
ray	rays	luxury	luxuries
storey	storeys	party	parties
trolley	trolleys	story	stories
turkey	turkeys	summary	summaries

b. Young <u>boys</u> cannot join <u>armies</u>.
   The <u>ladies</u> found the <u>books</u> in the <u>libraries</u>.
   I have <u>theories</u> about why <u>girls</u> <u>do</u> not play with the <u>toys</u>.
   The <u>monkeys</u> lived happily in the <u>valleys</u>.
   The <u>deputies</u> investigated the <u>robberies</u>.

c. enemy, spy, strawberry, company, gallery, fly, poppy

Exercise 4 Pages 42–43

a. one loaf   several <u>loaves</u>
   a <u>hoof</u>   four hooves
   the wolf   many <u>wolves</u>
   one <u>scarf</u>   two scarfs
   a thief   two <u>thieves</u>
   the chief   three <u>chiefs</u>
   one life   nine <u>lives</u>
   a <u>belief</u>   many beliefs
   one shelf   four <u>shelves</u>
   the reef   several <u>reefs</u>

b. dwarfs, elves, selves, sheaves

c. wives, calves, knives, wharves

d. After I cut ten apples in half, I had twenty <u>halves</u>.
<u>Gangs</u> of <u>thieves</u> steal cars in our <u>neighbourhoods</u>.
The <u>roofs</u> of the houses were damaged during the hurricane.
The <u>ladies</u> found the <u>cliffs</u> steep and difficult to climb.
The <u>leaves</u> fell from the <u>branches</u>.

Exercise 5 Page 44

a.

buffalo – buffaloes	banjo – banjos	halo – halos / haloes
cargo – cargoes	cello – cellos	mango – mangos / mangoes
domino – dominoes	curio – curios	memento – mementos /
echo – echoes	igloo – igloos	mementoes
hero – heroes	kilo – kilos	motto – mottos / mottoes
mosquito – mosquitoes	patio – patios	zero – zeros / zeroes
potato – potatoes	piano – pianos	
tomato – tomatoes	photo – photos	
tornado – tornadoes	radio – radios	
volcano – volcanoes	solo – solos	
	studio – studios	
	zoo – zoos	

b. Any sentences using the given words in their plural forms that show that
students understand their meanings, for example:
The children watched home videos showing their parents when they were
younger.
The orchestra played Beethoven's most famous concertos.
The famous football player was criticised for having so many tattoos.
The chef prepared avocados with prawns for the party.
Cowboys in America compete in rodeos throughout the year.

c. The <u>bellows</u> of the <u>buffaloes</u> scared the <u>mosquitoes</u>.
<u>Tornadoes</u> damaged the <u>crops</u> of <u>potatoes</u>, <u>tomatoes</u> and <u>mangoes / mangos</u>.
The talented <u>musicians</u> played the <u>pianos</u>, <u>cellos</u> and <u>banjos</u>.
I display <u>curios</u> and <u>mementos / mementoes</u> from the <u>trips</u> in my <u>studios</u>.
I wonder if <u>Eskimos</u> hang <u>photos</u> on the <u>walls</u> of the <u>igloos</u>.

d. The <u>echoes</u> rang out across the valley.

They always built <u>patios</u> around the houses they bought so they could sit outside and enjoy the view.

<u>Dominoes</u> is a fun game to play.

I feel sad when I see animals in cages at <u>zoos</u>.

Motorists listen to programmes broadcast on the <u>radios</u> in their cars.

Exercise 6 Pages 45–46

a.

one dice	several die
an aircraft	four aircraft
the cattle	many cattle
one goose	two geese
a man	two men
the child	three children
one ox	nine oxen
a buck	many buck
one pair of scissors	four pairs of scissors
one pair of trousers	five pairs of trousers

b. pliers, tweezers, lice, dice, barracks

c. They tapped their <u>feet</u> to the music.

There are millions of <u>fish</u> in the sea.

I had one <u>tooth</u> pulled out when I went to the dentist to have my <u>teeth</u> checked.

None of my <u>baggage</u> arrived at the airport so I had to buy new <u>clothes</u> to wear.

There was only one piece of <u>news</u> that I found interesting in the news broadcast.

Exercise 7 Page 47

a. Any three relevant examples for each rule, for example:

Add es or i to form the plural of nouns ending in us.

fungus – fungi

cactus – cacti

abacus – abacuses

Add x or s to form the plural of nouns ending in eau.

plateau – plateaus

gateau – gateaux

chateau – chateaux

Add e to form the plural of nouns ending in a.
formula – formulae
larva – larvae
vertebra – vertebrae

Change is to es to form the plural of nouns ending in is.
thesis – theses
axis – axes
hypothesis – hypotheses

b. Any sentences using the given words in their plural forms that show that
students understand their meanings, for example:
Parentheses (also known as brackets) are inserted around extra information in a
sentence.
The focuses / foci of this book are spelling and pronunciation.
The princesses danced with the beaus / beaux at the ball.
The gardener removed the algae from the pond.

Exercise 8 Pages 48–49

a.
backpacks	pancakes	daughters-in-law	lookers-on
boyfriends	rainbows	ladies-in-waiting	maids-of-honour
campfires	spoonfuls	runners-up	fathers-in-law
churchyards	stepfathers	passers-by	sisters-in-law
keyboards	stepmothers	editors-in-chief	
notebooks	wheelchairs		

b. water + melon = watermelon → watermelons
foot + print = footprint → footprints
week + end = weekend → weekends
pepper + mint= peppermint → peppermints
butter + fly = butterfly → butterflies
sun + flower = sunflower → sunflowers
base + ball = baseball → baseballs
pine + apple = pineapple → pineapples
grand + mother = grandmother → grandmothers
black + board = blackboard → blackboards
gentle + man = gentleman → gentlemen

c. Sons-in-law, Churchyards, Runners-up, Cheerleaders, Afternoons

d.
motel → motels	brunch → brunches
cheeseburger → cheeseburgers	interpol

19

e. Any five compound words with their correct plurals, for example:
chess + board = chessboard → chessboards
lap + top = laptop → laptops
lip + stick = lipstick → lipsticks
pen + knife = penknife → penknives
news + paper = newspaper → newspapers

Exercise 9 Pages 49–50

a.

mothers	books	formulae or formulas	waltzes
churches	dishes	octopi or octopuses	turkeys
parties	babies	oxen	chiefs
loaves	thieves	pianos	potatoes
echoes	zoos	beliefs	teeth
children	lice	plays	plateaux or plateaus
scissors	trousers	buses	sons-in-law
axes	runners-up	foxes	bosses

b. The police conducted <u>searches</u> for the <u>thieves</u> in the <u>bushes</u> near our <u>houses</u>.
The <u>men</u> strummed <u>tunes</u> on their <u>banjos</u>.
The <u>children</u> played the <u>pianos</u> at the music <u>concerts</u>.
The <u>deer</u> in the <u>countries</u> eat <u>leaves</u> from <u>trees</u>.
<u>Mice</u> gnawed the <u>corners</u> of the <u>photos</u> of my <u>heroes</u>.

c. Any sentences containing the correct plurals of the given words, for example:
Out of all the shows at the zoo, the ones with the kangaroos and the lionesses were the best.
The ladies were horrified when the monkeys stole the loaves of bread from their picnic.
The Seven Dwarfs always listened to radios on their journeys.
The hippopotamuses ate mangoes while carrying the rangers' baggage.
Whenever there are crises in churchyards, passers-by always assist.

d. Many sly <u>foxes</u> hide behind <u>bushes</u> and spy on <u>hens</u> laying <u>eggs</u>.
The <u>girls</u> wore <u>pyjamas</u> to the <u>parties</u>.
The <u>women</u> received <u>medals</u> because they were the <u>runners-up</u> in the <u>competitions</u>.
The <u>bookshelves</u> were loaded with <u>books, curios, photographs</u> and <u>mementos / mementoes</u>.
All the <u>women</u> baked <u>loaves</u> of bread to give to the many poor <u>people</u>.

e.	buffaloes	wolves	cockatoos	forks
	ponies	mice	wives	shoes
	monkeys	geese	loaves of bread	shampoos
	oxen	mosquitoes	potatoes	toothbrushes
	foxes	asses	knives	doves

Exercise 10 Pages 52–53

a. 1. altogether 6. precaution
   2. illogical 7. dissatisfied
   3. welfare 8. inexpensive
   4. irregular 9. displeased
   5. proceed 10. impossible

b.
detach	away, down, removing
antibiotic	against
uninspired	not
tripod	three
aerobatics	air
multiracial	many
postpone	after or later than
semicircle	half or partly
television	over a long distance, done by telephone, or on or for television
transport	across

c. The hunchback of Notre Dame was <u>misshapen</u>.
   The <u>misprint</u> in the advertisement led to confusion.
   I was <u>disappointed</u> with my spelling mark.
   His <u>mishap</u> made him miss the race.
   It is <u>illegal</u> to smoke on the school grounds.
   He went to hospital because his heart rate was <u>irregular</u>.
   If you <u>misspell</u> <u>illogical</u> I will know you did not learn your spelling words for the test.
   <u>Dissolve</u> the tablet in water.
   Although James and Matthew are brothers, they are quite <u>dissimilar</u>.
   Do not <u>unnerve</u> me by watching my every move.

d. cover, colour, agree, social, happy, please, cover, stand

Exercise 11 Page 54

a. Methods explained in question book on pages 2-10.

21

b. inaccurate, incapable, illegal, irregular, impossible, improbable, disappear, irrational, unemployed, misfortune, impatient, uninterested / disinterested, uninvolved, unneeded, misunderstand, displease

c. immobile, imperfect, incorrect, indirect, inattentive, infinite, incomplete, inconvenient

d. List of any words beginning with in- followed by five of these words used in sentences that show that students understand their meanings, for example:
There was **in**adequate food to feed the whole family.
He was **in**capable of writing neatly because his arm was broken.
There was **in**sufficient evidence to convict the criminal.
It is **in**decent to arrive at school naked.
The yacht sailed an **in**direct course to avoid the storm.

Exercise 12 Pages 55–56

a. Any two sentences containing a noun, adjective, verb and adverb from the list, for example:
The ambitious actor happily agreed to play the part of the homeless beggar.
The beautiful singer selfishly begged to perform the best songs.

b. The <u>woollen</u> scarf kept me warm.
The <u>selfish</u> child did not share.
The <u>homeless</u> beggar looked for shelter.
The famous <u>actor</u> visited our <u>neighbourhood</u>.
The congregation gave <u>generously</u> towards the collection.

c. 1. robber, liar, waiter, communicator, narrator
2. happily, smoothly, falsely, roughly, angrily
3. nervous, dangerous, joyous, spacious, melodious
4. sharpen, widen, harden, soften, loosen, lighten, weaken, tighten

d.

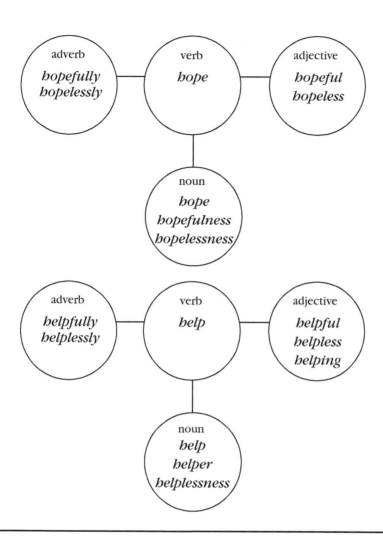

Exercise 13 Pages 58–59

a. heavy + ily, reply + ed, empty + ness, supply + er, carry + ed

b.

Verbs	+ ed	+ ing
study	studied	studying
marry	married	marrying
copy	copied	copying
pity	pitied	pitying
obey	obeyed	obeying
enjoy	enjoyed	enjoying

c. I picked an <u>armful</u> of <u>beautiful</u> flowers. My mother was <u>wonderfully</u> happy when I gave them to her. <u>Thankfully</u> she forgot my <u>awful</u> punishment.
She greeted everyone <u>cheerfully</u> while she walked the <u>playful</u> puppy.
He spoke <u>truthfully</u> at the <u>stressful</u> hearing.
The <u>boastful</u> man bragged <u>pitifully</u>.
A <u>spoonful</u> of honey will <u>hopefully</u> sweeten the bitter medicine.

d. **1.** treatment, replacement, argument, movement, settlement
2. useful, spiteful, colourful, careful, graceful
3. usefulness, spitefulness, colourfulness, carefulness, graciousness

e.

replied	replying
emptied	emptying
relayed	relaying
obeyed	obeying
pitied	pitying

f. The <u>excited</u> children <u>hiked</u> up the mountain without <u>noticing</u> its <u>steepness</u>. At the top <u>stillness</u> overcame the group as they <u>admired</u> the <u>amazingly</u> beautiful view. The <u>enjoyment</u> experienced on that day <u>filled</u> them with <u>gladness</u>. The rest of the students were <u>envious</u> and <u>hoped</u> / <u>hopeful</u> they would also have the opportunity to go on the <u>outing</u>.

Exercise 14 Page 60

a.

	+ er	+ est	+ ness
wet	wetter	wettest	wetness
hot	hotter	hottest	hotness
flat	flatter	flattest	flatness
thin	thinner	thinnest	thinness
big	bigger	biggest	bigness

b. grinned, boyhood, fitted/fitment, payment, stepped

c. flatter, flatly; hotter, hotly; madder, madly; sadder, sadly

d. Any sentence using three words from the list, for example:
The joyful child hopped down the street until she slipped on a banana skin.

Exercise 15 Page 61

a. alter + tion = alteration
begin + ing = beginning
benefit + ed = benefited
carpet + ing = carpeting
comfort + able = comfortable
commit + ed = committed
council + or = councillor
forbid + en = forbidden
forget + ing = forgetting
forgot + en = forgotten
gallop + ing = galloping
garden + er = gardener
limit + ed = limited
murmur + ing = murmuring
occur + ed = occurred
omit + ed = omitted
profit + able = profitable
refer + ing = referring
regret + able = regrettable
target + ing = targeting

b. forgetting, forbidding, permitting, quarrelled, compelling, marvellous

c. **en**tered, **or**dered, **lim**ited, **mar**keted, **par**doned

d. Any sentence using three words from the list, for example:
Forgetting the beginning of the speech, the actor omitted the first few sentences.

e. referred   galloped
forgotten   beginning
carpeted   regretted
forbidding   gardening

Exercise 16 Page 62

a.
boiled	labelled	quarrelled	schooled
controlled	mailed	railed	sealed
failed	modelled	rebelled	soiled
faired	parcelled	revealed	
fouled	patrolled	rivalled	
fulfilled	propelled	sailed	

b. As we <u>travelled</u> across the country we <u>marvelled</u> at the beautiful scenery.
The children <u>revealed</u> creative talent while <u>modelling</u> the clay.
He <u>cancelled</u> his <u>sailing</u> trip.
The shiny <u>metallic</u> car was <u>stealing</u> the limelight.
The students <u>rebelled</u> against the high <u>failure</u> rate.

c. The police <u>patrolled</u> the area.
The <u>sailing</u> clubs <u>quarrelled</u> about the foul.
He <u>fouled</u> the goalkeeper and was sent off the field.
She <u>sealed</u> the parcel and <u>mailed</u> it across the country.
In <u>fairness</u> to the students, school should close when it is <u>boiling</u> hot like this.

Exercise 17 Page 63

a. Dying means likely to die soon (from to die).
Dyeing means changing the colour of something (from to dye).

b. Drop the silent e when the suffix begins with a vowel: exciting, engaging, hoping, replacing survival
Keep the silent e when the suffix begins with a consonant: engagement, excitement, immediately, replacement, politely
Keep the silent e when the suffixes -able and -ous are added to words that contain a soft g or c: courageous, manageable, noticeable, outrageous
Keep the silent e when the word may be mistaken for another word: dyeing
Keep the silent e when adding -age to the words line and mile: lineage, mileage
To add a suffix to a word ending in ie drop the e and change the i to y: dying, lying

c. facing, inviting, tying, noting, providing, reducing, polluting, inviting, smoking, increasing

d. tribal, arrival, recital, tidal, bridal, approval, removal, refusal, universal, natural

e. We enjoyed <u>tying</u> and <u>dyeing</u> our t-shirts.
It was <u>outrageous</u> how many children were <u>lying</u>.
The disease is <u>cured</u> / <u>curable</u>.
He damaged his <u>spinal</u> column in the accident.
The book was <u>surprisingly</u> good.
Her accuracy when <u>calculating</u> is <u>notable</u>.

Exercise 18 Page 64

a. frolic + ing = frolicking   traffic + ing = trafficking   logic + ly = logically
mimic + ing = mimicking academic + ly = academically medic + ly = medically
panic + ing = panicking   energetic + ly = energetically pathetic + ly = pathetically
picnic + ing = picnicking

b. picnicked, trafficked, mimicked, frolicked, panicked

c. Any sentences using the given words + -ly, which show that students understand
their meaning, for example:
Fabrice Muamba was clinically dead for 78 minutes following his collapse during
a football match.
The clown comically tripped over his suitcase.
Tragically, the clown injured himself when falling over.
Ebooks allow you to read dynamically, with added resources.
The climber was dramatically rescued from the mountain after she became
trapped on a narrow ledge.

Exercise 19 Page 65

a. abst<u>ai</u>n
app<u>ea</u>r
av<u>oi</u>d
compl<u>ai</u>n
desp<u>ai</u>r
det<u>ai</u>n
entert<u>ai</u>n
expl<u>ai</u>n
expl<u>oi</u>t
hon<u>ou</u>r
rem<u>ai</u>n
rep<u>ai</u>r

b. despaired – despairing   complained – complaining
entertained – entertaining   avoided – avoiding
appeared – appearing   detained – detaining
explained – explaining   abstained – abstaining
honoured – honouring   remained – remaining
repaired – repairing   exploited – exploiting

c. favourable, fashionable, honourable, repairable, explainable

d. flavoured, regretting, traveller, laboured, musically, picnicking, national, favourable, repelling, cautioned

e. I <u>despaired</u> when my mother <u>commented</u> on my appearance again. I have <u>explained</u> that it is <u>fashionable</u>, but she has not <u>abstained</u> from <u>commenting</u>. <u>Maintaining</u> my stylish reputation is <u>becoming</u> more and more difficult.

Exercise 20 Pages 65–66

a.
1. hopeful	**8.** bagful	**14.** courageous
2. beautiful	**9.** slipped	**15.** panicking
3. reliable	**10.** referring	**16.** comically
4. heavily	**11.** forbidden	**17.** tried
5. likeable	**12.** benefited	**18.** lying
6. emptiness	**13.** dying	**19.** curable
7. argument		

b. impossible, uncommon, inexperienced, illiterate, disrespect

c.

	+ ed	+ ing
convey	conveyed	conveying
rely	relied	relying
deny	denied	denying
hope	hoped	hoping
obey	obeyed	obeying
pity	pitied	pitying

d.
immovable	irregularity
dissolvable	illogical
alright	precautionary
dishonestly	displeased
illegally	unemployment

Word endings
Exercise 1 Pages 67–68

a. strategic, chronic, ethnic, static

b. comic, fantastic, panic, static

c. strategically, fantastically, comically, chronically

d. acoustic – relating to sound or hearing, authentic – real, aerobic – relating to oxygen, ceramic – made from clay, eccentric – strange or unusual

e. Dear <u>Nick</u>

We had a <u>fantastic</u> time on our <u>scientific</u> exploration to the <u>Arctic</u> Ocean. There were no crowds or <u>hectic</u> <u>traffic</u> in sight. We enjoyed researching the <u>topic</u> and are very happy that there was not a <u>horrific</u> accident. It was <u>tragic</u> that Rick's mother died while he was away.

It was a pity that you were <u>sick</u> and missed out on this <u>magical</u> trip. Hopefully you will be able to join us next time. Start taking a <u>tonic</u> now so you are healthy and <u>energetic</u>.

Regards
Eric

f. Any three sentences using several words from the list, for example:
Her brother was sick, with chronic back pain, which made him panic.
The traffic was static in the thick fog.
The comic actor hit his car with a stick and gave it a kick.

Exercise 2 Page 69

a.

comfortable	possible
edible	reasonable
fashionable	reliable
flexible	resistible
honourable	sensible
horrible	sociable
irritable	terrible
manageable	visible

b. 'Resistible' breaks the rule that if you remove the ending you are usually not left with a complete word.
'Irritable' breaks the rule that if you remove the ending you are usually left with a complete word.

c. flexible, reliable, sociable

d. <u>reason</u>able, <u>comfort</u>able, <u>manage</u>able, <u>fashion</u>able, <u>honour</u>able, <u>resist</u>ible, <u>flex</u>ible

e. impossible, inedible, invisible, irresistible, inflexible, illegible

f. edible, sociable, flexible, visible, honourable

g. sociable, possible, reliable, visible, honourable, flexible, edible, resistible, reasonable, fashionable

---

Exercise 3 Pages 70–71

a. altar, lunar

b. Any words ending in –lar, for example:

angular	dollar	molecular	scholar
binocular	exemplar	muscular	secular
bipolar	funicular	particular	similar
burglar	granular	pedlar	singular
cellar	insular	perpendicular	solar
cellular	irregular	polar	spectacular
circular	jocular	poplar	stellar
collar	modular	popular	tabular
consular	molar	regular	vehicular

c. explorer
editor
author
narrator
scholar

d. minister, similar, cellar, spectator, regular

e. owner, visitor, narrator, reporter, listener, fighter

f. lunar, regular, fighter, cellar, popular, minister, father, editor, solar, author

g. operator, collector, similar, muscular, spectacular, composer, stranger, cellular, equator, treasurer

Exercise 4 Page 72

a.

-ant	-ance	-ent	-ence
brilliant	acceptance	competent	competence
elegant	advance	continent	conference
important	assistance	different	confidence
radiant	brilliance	frequent	difference
significant	elegance	urgent	reference
	importance		
	radiance		
	relevance		
	significance		

b. Any five sentences using adjectives from the list, for example:
There is a frequent train service between London and Paris.
The bride wore an elegant gown of taffeta.
Barack Obama made a moving acceptance speech when he won the US election.
The boss sent an urgent memo to her workforce.
The significance of the goalkeeper to his team cannot be underestimated.

c. difference, importance, confidence, radiance, intelligence

d. important, significant, elegant, magnificent, persistent

e. indifferent, unimportant, insignificant, infrequent, unconfident

f. Any sentences using the given pairs of words, for example:
The importance of Antarctica as a continent is due to its ice, which reflects heat from the sun back into the atmosphere.
The elegant bride shone with radiance in her beautiful gown.
The competent businessman showed his brilliance in closing the deal.

Exercise 5 Pages 73–74

a. & b.

-ary	-ery
bound<u>a</u>ry	brav<u>e</u>ry
diction<u>a</u>ry	brib<u>e</u>ry
element<u>a</u>ry	cemet<u>e</u>ry
Febru<u>a</u>ry	deliv<u>e</u>ry
imagin<u>a</u>ry	discov<u>e</u>ry
libr<u>a</u>ry	jewell<u>e</u>ry
liter<u>a</u>ry	nurs<u>e</u>ry
necess<u>a</u>ry	qu<u>e</u>ry
prim<u>a</u>ry	slav<u>e</u>ry
second<u>a</u>ry	station<u>e</u>ry
station<u>a</u>ry	surg<u>e</u>ry
tempor<u>a</u>ry	
terti<u>a</u>ry	

c. elementary, primary, secondary, tertiary

d. query, library, nursery, temporary, necessary

e. discovery, stationery, cemetery, literary, stationary, bravery, surgery, boundary

f. When <u>slavery</u> was abolished people were given their freedom.
I received a special <u>delivery</u> on my birthday.
The author received a special <u>literary</u> award.
<u>February</u> is the shortest month.
It is against the law to be involved in <u>bribery</u> and corruption.

g. jewel, diction

Exercise 6 Pages 74–75

a.

-acle nouns	-cal adjectives	-icle nouns
obstacle	practical	vehicle
spectacle	identical	article
tentacle	physical	icicle
miracle	topical	particle
oracle	vertical	
	logical	
	focal	

b. long, thin arm of a sea creature
long, pointed stick of ice
priest or priestess
a small piece of something
standing upright

c. practical, identical

d. Any sentences using the given pairs of words, for example:
It can be more practical to walk than use a vehicle.
No icicle is identical to another.
The topical chat show described the actor's escape from his wrecked
car as a miracle.

e. phys • i • cal, prac • ti • cal, i • den • ti • cal

f. It was a <u>miracle</u> that he did not break his neck in the diving accident.
On New Year's Eve we watched a <u>spectacle</u> of fireworks.

g. 1. vehicle
2. identical
3. oracle
4. vertical
5. spectacle

Exercise 7 Page 76

a. recede, precede, exceed, accede, proceed, succeed, concede, cede, supersede, intercede

b. precede, concede, succeed, accede

c.

1. precede	**6.** recede
2. proceed	**7.** cede
3. intercede	**8.** concede
4. succeed	**9.** supersede
5. secede	**10.** exceed

d. concede, accede, supersede, recede, intercede, exceed, proceed, succeed, precede, cede

---

Exercise 8 Pages 77–78

a.

-al	-el	-le
rural	panel	idle
principal	jewel	ample
local	label	riddle
signal	hostel	eagle
survival	model	sample
professional	parcel	example
personal	novel	chuckle
national	snorkel	title
	rebel	
	scalpel	
	kennel	
	cancel	

b. chuckle, snorkel, national, cancel, sample, survival, idle, label, professional, hostel, ample

c. idled, labelled, sampled, rebelled, chuckled, cancelled, knifed

d. idle, local, title, label, riddle, panel

e. True
False. Farms are usually found in rural areas.
True
True
False. Private relates to personal affairs.

f. 1. normal   5. invisible
    2. settle   6. possible
    3. equal   7. camel
    4. general   8. travel

Exercise 9 Page 79

a. If a word ending sounds like shun, it is probably spelt -tion.
    If a word ending sounds a bit like zhin, it is probably spelt -sion.
    Drop the final e before adding -sion or -tion, for example decorate → decoration.
    Drop the final de from words that end in these letters, for example decide → decision.
    Drop the final e and add a to words that end in ve, for example observe → observation.

b. explosion, fusion, exclusion, inclusion, erosion

c.
Verbs	Nouns
decorate	decoration
collide	collision
observe	observation
confuse	confusion
quote	quotation
decide	decision
locate	location
revise	revision
navigate	navigation
televise	television
refrigerate	refrigeration
conclude	conclusion

d. location
    station
    observation
    television
    vision
    caution
    navigation
    refrigeration

e. We will decorate the tree with green and red <u>decorations</u>.

After studying the problem for hours, I have come to the <u>conclusion</u> it cannot be solved.

Luckily no one was hurt in the <u>collision</u>, but it caused a traffic jam.

You need to <u>revise</u> your spelling rules before the test.

At the sound of the fire alarm <u>confusion</u> broke out as everyone fled in different directions.

I cannot decide whether I should study or watch <u>television</u>.

The <u>quotation</u> for the building alterations was very high.

You must plant trees to help prevent soil <u>erosion</u>.

Exercise 10 Pages 80–81

a.

-ere	-ier	-eer
ad<u>here</u>	<u>amp</u>lifier	<u>car</u>eer
hemi<u>sphere</u>	<u>ang</u>rier	ch<u>eer</u>
in<u>since</u>re	<u>bar</u>rier	<u>engine</u>er
inter<u>fer</u>e	<u>car</u>rier	jeer
pers<u>eve</u>re	<u>cash</u>ier	<u>peer</u>
re<u>ve</u>re	<u>fron</u>tier	sneer
s<u>eve</u>re	<u>pier</u>	veer
sincere	<u>tier</u>	volun<u>teer</u>

b. volunteer, hemisphere, persevere, barrier, interfere, amplifier, sincere, engineer

c. Any sentences using peer and pier that demonstrate their meaning:
   pier – a structure that sticks out into the sea
   peer – to look carefully or a person who is an equal

d. frontier
   veer
   severe
   adhere
   insincere
   revere

e. volunteer
   auctioneer
   pioneer
   puppeteer
   mountaineer
   overseer

f. cashier, tier, career, angrier, sneer, carrier

Exercise 11 Page 82

a.

-ought	-aught	-ough sounds like oh	-ough sounds like oo	-ough sounds like ow	-ough sounds like uff
ought	caught	although	through	plough	tough
bought	distraught	dough		drought	rough
brought	taught				enough
fought	onslaught				
sought	fraught				
nought					
thought					

b. a powerful attack, very worried, a farming tool for digging fields, looked for

c. Any sentences using the given sets of words, for example:
   1. I caught a cold when the fisherman taught me to catch fish on the rough sea.
   2. Although the meat was very tough, the butcher fought hard to cut it.
   3. After losing her fifth game of noughts and crosses, "Enough!" she thought. "I'm playing draughts!"
   4. Although she ought to have bought a cake, instead she brought ice cream to the party.

d. My teacher <u>taught</u> me how to spell supercalifragilisticexpialidocious.
   I slithered <u>through</u> the dark narrow tunnel.
   I kneaded the <u>dough</u> to make bread.

e. bought, sought, thought, rough, enough, nought, taught,
   caught, distraught, onslaught, through, dough, plough,
   brought, fought, although

Exercise 12 Pages 83–84

a.

-ous	-ious	-eous
enormous	anxious	courageous
famous	cautious	gorgeous
generous	delicious	piteous
humorous	gracious	
jealous	luxurious	
monstrous	obvious	
perilous	pious	
	precious	
	previous	
	serious	

b. The poor hungry puppy had a <u>piteous</u> whine.
The <u>courageous</u> man risked his life to rescue the child.
The <u>famous</u> movie star lived in a <u>luxurious</u> mansion.
We found the comedian very <u>humorous</u>.
It was <u>obvious</u> that the <u>gorgeous</u> girl would win the beauty contest.

c. serious, jealous, anxious, cautious, enormous

d. generous, previous, gracious, precious, cautious

e. Any descriptive sentence using monstrous, for example:
The monstrous traffic jam outside the airport caused the businessman to miss his flight.

f. piteous, famous, monstrous, serious, generous, jealous, gorgeous, humorous, delicious, luxurious, enormous, obvious, courageous, anxious, previous, gracious, cautious, precious

---

Exercise 13 Pages 84–85

a. Any two sentences containing meanwhile and worthwhile that explain their meaning, for example:
My father went to my mother's office to meet her; meanwhile, she went to his office to meet him.
She left her job as a lawyer to become a charity worker, which she felt was a more worthwhile career.

b. He made a <u>futile</u> attempt to catch his <u>mobile</u> phone before it fell into the water.
If you <u>compile</u> a <u>file</u> of all your important notes you will find it easier to study.
A <u>crocodile</u> and a lizard are scaly <u>reptiles</u>.

c. fragile   vile
    volatile   mobile
    smile

d. agility, futility, volatility, fragility, mobility

e.

Word	Plural	Past tense	+ ing
file	files	filed	filing
tile	tiles	tiled	tiling
smile	smiles	smiled	smiling
compile		compiled	compiling
textile	textiles		
missile	missiles		

f. smile, volatile, agile, compile, mobile, meanwhile, versatile,
worthwhile, reptile, fragile, missile, futile, crocodile, textile

Exercise 14 Pages 85–86

a. The underlined words may vary as some words contain more than one
small word.

argu<u>ment</u>   <u>environ</u>ment

<u>attach</u>ment   expe<u>rim</u>ent

ce<u>ment</u>   f<u>rag</u>ment

com<u>ment</u>   impro<u>ve</u>ment

com<u>mit</u>ment   <u>in</u> <u>strum</u>ent

compli<u>ment</u>   <u>manage</u>ment

disap<u>point</u>ment   <u>pay</u>ment

docu<u>ment</u>   <u>require</u>ment

ele<u>ment</u>   seg<u>ment</u>

en<u>joy</u>ment   <u>state</u>ment

b. Definitions should be similar to the following:
argument – disagreement
attachment – something that can be added
cement – mixed with water and sand to make concrete
comment – something that expresses your opinion
commitment – dedication to a cause or activity

c. segment, requirement, improvement, compliment, enjoyment

d. Please read the important <u>document</u> from the <u>management</u> of the company.
A tiny <u>fragment</u> of the china cup chipped off when I knocked it against the sink.
The <u>element</u> in my kettle is broken so I have to boil water on the stove.
The bank sent me a <u>statement</u> which showed how much money was in the account.
We used the <u>instrument</u> to perform a science <u>experiment</u>.

e. The winning team experienced great <u>excitement</u>, but the losing team moaned with <u>disappointment</u>.
There has been a huge <u>improvement</u> in your marks this term.
Your <u>commitment</u> to <u>improvement</u> has been admirable.
The <u>argument</u> lead to a break in the <u>agreement</u>.
The <u>enjoyment</u> experienced by the students on camp was talked about for days.

f. cement, management, enjoyment, segment, statement,
fragment, disappointment, compliment, comment,
improvement, document, requirement, element, argument,
attachment, compliment, instrument, experiment

Exercise 15 Pages 87–88

a. true
clues
glue
rescue
subdue
tissue

b. I <u>construe</u> his silence to mean that he is happy for us to go.
<u>Continue</u> walking along the <u>avenue</u> until you see a stone <u>statue</u> in front of a park.
The <u>venue</u> is ideal for a music concert.
I hope we do not have to stand in a long <u>queue</u> for tickets.
I will <u>pursue</u> a career in marketing.

c. queue, continue, pursue, venue

d. blue, due

e. Any sentences showing the meanings of the homophones blew – blue, dew – due, for example:
The strong wind <u>blew</u> the clouds across the <u>blue</u> sky.
The grass was still damp with <u>dew</u> when the postman was <u>due</u> to deliver the parcel.

f. Any sentences using the given words in different ways, for example:
The actor used <u>cue</u> cards to help him learn his lines.
The picture was a <u>cue</u> to help the reader make sense of the text.

The librarian will <u>issue</u> the books.
We should raise the <u>issue</u> of graffiti at the next council meeting.

I have nothing of <u>value</u>.
My family <u>values</u> truth and honesty.

I feel <u>blue</u>.
I like the colour <u>blue</u>.

I want to <u>pursue</u> a career in science.
The police decided to <u>pursue</u> the van as it looked suspicious.

g. due, tissue, construe, blue, glue, venue, value, queue, avenue, rescue, statue, cue, true, pursue, subdue, continue, clue, issue

---

Exercise 16 Pages 88–89

a.

ac • ces • so • rise	civ • i • lise	en • er • gise	sum • ma • rise
ad • ver • tise	col • o • nise	ex • er • cise	su • per • vise
ag • o • nise	crit • i • cise	fa • mil • iar • ise	te • le • vise
a • pol • o • gise	de • vise	i • dol • ise	vic • tim • ise
bap • tise	em • pha • sise	or • gan • ise	vis • u • al • ise

b. the / an accessory, the / a baptism, the / a civilisation, the / a colony, the / an idol, the / an emphasis

c. apologise
emphasise
supervise
criticise
advertise
visualise
exercise
devise
organise

d. energise, agonise, summarise, familiarise, visualise, apologise

e. devise, exercise, energise, accessorise, advertise, colonise,
baptise, emphasise, civilise, criticise, summarise, familiarise,
idolise, visualise, supervise, organise, apologise, agonise

Exercise 17 Pages 89–90

a.

-ive pronounced as in alive	-ive pronounced as in active
alive	active
survive	creative
arrive	forgive
connive	captive
contrive	adjective
jive	massive
strive	expensive
thrive	digestive
	constructive
	attractive
	positive
	destructive
	competitive
	passive
	sensitive
	negative

b. The <u>creative</u> artist bought <u>expensive</u> oil paints.
To <u>survive</u> in the desert you had better <u>strive</u> to make your water last.
The <u>captive</u> hoped to <u>contrive</u> an escape plan.
The <u>competitive</u> quote won the company a <u>massive</u> contract.
The <u>active</u> toddler will <u>arrive</u> and keep us running all day.

c. Any sentences containing the antonyms thrive – survive, destructive – constructive, positive – negative that show that students understand their meanings, for example:

Lemurs <u>thrive</u> in the rainforest.
Lemurs barely <u>survive</u> in areas where their habitat is destroyed.

Superstorm Sandy was one of the most <u>destructive</u> storms in recent times.
The teacher's <u>constructive</u> criticism of her students' essays helped them to improve their work.

The policeman was <u>positive</u> that the man he was questioning was the culprit.
When I asked my parents if I could stay out late on a school night, their answer was <u>negative</u>.

d. <u>Forgive</u> and forget   Dead or <u>alive</u>

e. adjective
sensitive
jive
thrive
digestive
attractive

f. creativity, captivity, positivity, passivity, sensitivity, negativity

g. adjective, massive, destructive, competitive, strive, thrive, connive, alive, active, creative, survive, forgive, arrive, captive, constructive, jive, attractive, positive, passive, sensitive, negative, expensive, digestive, contrive

Exercise 18 Pages 91–92

a.
ab • stract	col • lect	ex • tinct	ob • struct
act	con • flict	ex • tract	pact
ad • dict	con • struct	im • pact	pre • dict
af • fect	con • tract	in • stinct	pro • duct
ar • chi • tect	de • duct	in • struct	sub • tract
at • tract	de • fect	ne • glect	tact

b. addiction, attraction, construction, extraction

c. Various answers are possible, for example:
Practise reading an <u>extract</u> of the story aloud.
The dentist is going to <u>extract</u> four of my teeth.

When a government passes a Bill it becomes an <u>Act</u>.
The children loved to <u>act</u> in their school play.

The negotiator resolved the <u>conflict</u> with soothing words.
I do not know who to believe because the accounts of the driver of the car and the eyewitness <u>conflict</u>.

The sweetshop's best-selling <u>product</u> is the chocolate-covered fudge.
The <u>product</u> of 5 and 3 is 15.

I had to <u>collect</u> my thoughts and calmly tell the officer what happened.
I <u>collect</u> newspapers from my neighbours for our recycling project.

The author signed the <u>contract</u> and returned it to the publisher.
I hope I do not <u>contract</u> an infectious disease while I am in the Amazon.

d. diplomacy → tact
hinder → obstruct
agreement → pact
entice → attract
teach → instruct
forecast → predict
build → construct
fetch → collect

e. subtract, defect, neglect, extinct, abstract

f. If you subtract the product of 2 and 12 from 100, the answer is <u>76</u>.
If you deduct 10 from the product of 7 and 8 the answer is <u>46</u>.
If you become a television <u>addict</u> it will impact on your life in a negative way and <u>affect</u> your friendships.
The architect relies on knowledge and <u>instinct</u> when designing buildings.

g. neglect, act, instruct, tact, detect, instinct, pact, architect,
conflict, extract, construct, addict, subtract, extinct,
product, contract, predict, affect, effect, attract, impact,
obstruct, abstract, collect

Exercise 19 Pages 92–93

a. Students will underline different part of the words depending on what they find tricky.

actual	equal	manual	unusual
annual	factual	mutual	virtual
casual	gradual	perpetual	visual
contextual	individual	punctual	
dual	intellectual	spiritual	

b. Look at the <u>contextual</u> clues to work out the meanings of words.
You do not have to be highly <u>intellectual</u> to achieve good marks.
We have a <u>mutual</u> agreement to respect one another.
A <u>spiritual</u> leader from America spoke at our church.
I have never seen anything as <u>unusual</u> as that statue.
It is important to be <u>punctual</u> for the meeting.
The <u>actual</u> budget is printed in a <u>manual</u> and discussed at the <u>annual</u> meeting.

c. virtual – almost, perpetual – continuing for ever, dual – with two parts

d.

casual	→	informal
equal	→	identical
factual	→	accurate
gradual	→	slow
individual	→	separate
visual	→	optical

e. unusually, perpetually, spiritually, annually, visually, gradually

f. actual, annual, casual, contextual, dual, equal, factual, gradual, individual, intellectual, manual, mutual, perpetual, punctual, spiritual, unusual, virtual, visual

Exercise 20 Page 94

a.

abacus	census	eucalyptus	platypus
apparatus	chorus	focus	status
asparagus	circus	fungus	surplus
cactus	consensus	minus	virus
campus	discus	octopus	walrus

b. Three animals: octopus, platypus, walrus
Four plants: asparagus, cactus, eucalyptus, fungus

45

c. choruses, circuses, discuses, octopuses or octopi, statuses, viruses

d. Any synonyms for the given words, for example:

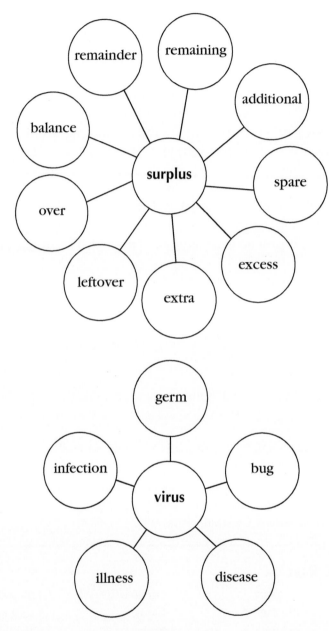

e. The <u>focus</u> on <u>campus</u> this term has been to get a <u>consensus</u> about whether or not the <u>platypus</u> should appear <u>minus</u> its bill.

f. asparagus, cactus, campus, census, chorus, circus, consensus, discus, eucalyptus, focus, fungus, minus, octopus, platypus, status, surplus, virus, walrus

Sneaky letters

Exercise 1 Page 95

accurately, achievement, advertisement, arguing, arrangement, before, completely, different, divinity, duly, forceful, hopeful, interested, judging, politeness, tasteless, truly, usage

Exercise 2 Page 97

a. tom<u>b</u>, bo<u>a</u>rd, <u>ais</u>le, su<u>bt</u>le, Tu<u>e</u>sday, hym<u>n</u>, <u>w</u>ho<u>l</u>e, <u>h</u>e<u>ig</u>ht, solem<u>n</u>, condem<u>n</u>, <u>p</u>sy<u>ch</u>ologist, ans<u>w</u>er, vag<u>ue</u> , <u>g</u>uest, this<u>tl</u>e

b. honesty, doubt, thumb, numb, hour, knuckle, knowledge, wrong, knives, kneel, hymn, scholar, sword, climber, wrist, muscle, pseudonym, Wednesday, raspberry

Exercise 3 Pages 98–99

a.

ac • cel • er • ate	ac • cor • di • on	cap • puc • cin • os	oc • cu • py
ac • cent	ac • count	des • ic • cat • ed	oc • cur
ac • cept	ac • coun • tant	ec • cen • tric	pre • oc • cu
ac • cess	ac • cum • u • late	hic • cup	• pied
ac • ci • dent	ac • cu • rate	moc • ca • sin	rac • coon
ac • claim	ac • cuse	oc • ca • sion	soc • cer
ac • com • mo • da • tion	ac • cus • tomed	oc • ca • sion • al • ly	suc • cess
	broc • co • li	oc • cu • pa • tion	suc • cumb
ac • com • plish			vac • ci • na • tion

b.

hiccup	→	a gulping sound
cappuccino	→	milky coffee with froth
moccasin	→	a flat leather shoe
accelerate	→	to go increasingly quickly
succumb	→	to give in to something
broccoli	→	a vegetable
accent	→	a way of pronouncing words
accountant	→	a person who works with financial records
acclaim	→	to praise someone highly
accordion	→	a musical instrument

47

c. desiccated   →   dried
    eccentric   →   unusual
    accident   →   crash
    accomplish   →   achieve
    accept   →   receive
    accumulate   →   gather
    access   →   entry
    occasionally   →   sometimes
    accustomed   →   familiar
    occur   →   happen

d. We are looking for <u>accommodation</u> to <u>occupy</u> for the entire summer holiday.
They need an <u>accurate</u> goal scorer in their <u>soccer</u> team if they want to achieve
more <u>success</u>.
She took the baby to the clinic to get her <u>vaccination</u>.
Do you have an <u>account</u> at a bank?
Do not <u>accuse</u> me of cheating.
We are celebrating a special <u>occasion</u>.
I hope I have an interesting <u>occupation</u> when I grow up.

e. Any sentences that show that students understand the meaning of the ten words
chosen, for example:
I hope the plane doesn't <u>accelerate</u> so quickly that I am pushed back in my seat.
The Irish boxer speaks with a beautiful <u>accent</u>.
"I <u>accept</u>," gushed the princess, when the prince asked her to marry him.
<u>Access</u> to the internet is free in most libraries.
Following a road <u>accident</u>, my friend had a bruise on his arm.
The actress received critical <u>acclaim</u> for her portrayal of a famous politician.
Our holiday <u>accommodation</u> was disappointing, as it was cold, damp and far
from the beach.
After years of trying, this is the year I hope to finally <u>accomplish</u> grade 6 at the
piano.
The <u>accordion</u> player busks outside the station.
My cousin and her new husband have opened a joint bank <u>account</u>.
My sister likes working with money so has decided to become an <u>accountant</u>.
Will we be able to open the door tomorrow if snow continues to <u>accumulate</u>
in our garden overnight?
My new watch is <u>accurate</u> to the nearest second.
Do not <u>accuse</u> me of stealing from your stall.
Despite being <u>accustomed</u> to hot weather, Jan felt faint in the sun.
My little brother doesn't like <u>broccoli</u> but always eats his cauliflower.

"I'll have three <u>cappuccinos</u>, two lattes and a black coffee, please," requested the first customer at my coffee shop.

<u>Desiccated</u> coconut is my favourite sweet treat.

My <u>eccentric</u> uncle insisted on wearing a sunhat even in winter.

Despite holding her breath, receiving a large shock and drinking from the opposite side of the cup, Karen's continued to <u>hiccup</u>.

I found my missing <u>moccasin</u> under my bed so now I can wear a comfortable pair of shoes again.

Christmas was just the right <u>occasion</u> for my grandmother to wear her new hat.

<u>Occasionally</u>, I enjoy a chocolate biscuit with my cup of tea.

School leavers must consider which <u>occupation</u> they wish to pursue.

How is it possible for the menswear department to <u>occupy</u> the entire ground floor of the large shop?

The keen astronomer gazed at the sky waiting for the lunar eclipse to <u>occur</u>.

<u>Preoccupied</u> with her money worries, the driver lost concentration and swerved off the road.

The <u>raccoon</u> is a grey mammal found mainly in North America.

In some countries, football is known as <u>soccer</u>.

The manager achieved great <u>success</u> with his new football team.

I think that after treating many patients, the doctor may <u>succumb</u> to the flu.

The baby had his <u>vaccination</u> against measles, mumps and rubella.

Exercise 4 Pages 99–100

a.

whiff	→	smell
ruffle	→	unsettle
offering	→	contribution
efficient	→	well-organised
difficult	→	hard
affectionate	→	demonstrative
affable	→	pleasant
affix	→	attach
baffle	→	confuse
affair	→	matter

b. Definitions should be similar to the following:

offence – crime

official – relating to a position of responsibility

scaffold – a structure to reach high parts of a building

graffiti – words or drawings in public places

sufficient – enough

c. The <u>effect</u> of the robbery <u>affected</u> us for ages.

Get <u>off</u> the table and sit on your chair.

The dealers were <u>trafficking</u> goods illegally.

My father works in an <u>office</u> that overlooks the sea.

I like the new girl as she is very <u>affable</u>.

d. I was standing on the <u>scaffold</u> drawing <u>graffiti</u> on the wall when an <u>officer</u> of the law stopped and told me I was committing a criminal <u>offence</u>. He gave me an <u>official</u> warning. I was thankful as I could not have <u>afforded</u> to pay a fine. I was <u>sufficiently</u> embarrassed by the whole <u>affair</u>. Next time I am bored I will make sure I do something <u>different</u>. Perhaps I should stay at home and drink <u>coffee</u>. My friends <u>scoffed</u> at my stupidity.

e. Any sentences using the given sets of three words, for example:

I despise people who cause the suffering of wild animals like the buffalo, giraffe and rhinoceros.

It would baffle me if my workmate declared he despised the whiff of coffee.

My father is in hospital because he fell off a high scaffold into oncoming traffic.

Exercise 5 Pages 101–102

a. accidentally, fulfilled, jewellery, marvellous, occasionally, propeller, usually

b.

	+ ed	+ ing
allow	allowed	allowing
challenge	challenged	challenging
gallop	galloped	galloping
recall	recalled	recalling
recollect	recollected	recollecting
swallow	swallowed	swallowing

c. accidentally   →   not on purpose

bullet   →   ammunition used in a gun

gorilla   →   a large ape

millennium   →   1000 years

seagull   →   you see these flying over the sea looking for fish

caterpillar   →   this turns into a moth

umbrella   →   you need this in the rain

villain   →   an evil character
college   →   a place to study
valley   →   a low-lying area between mountains

d. dull, shallow, intelligent, recall, occasionally

e. I went to the art <u>gallery</u> to see the exhibition.
The lines in a parallelogram run <u>parallel</u>.
I would prefer living in a small <u>village</u> compared to a big city.
Can you <u>recollect/recall</u> whether or not you have met her before?
My mother does not <u>allow</u> me to <u>swallow</u> bubble gum.

Exercise 6 Pages 102–103

a. Definitions should be similar to the following:
gimmick – a trick to attract attention
mammal – an animal that gives birth to its babies
summit – an important meeting or the highest point
committee – a group that represents a larger group
hammock – a bed tied up between two ends

b. immature   →   childish
accommodate   →   house
immense   →   vast
command   →   order
shimmer   →   gleam
commence   →   start
summon   →   call
immune   →   resistant
immediate   →   instantaneous
mammoth   →   huge

c. I <u>recommend</u> that you <u>commit</u> yourself to following a <u>swimming</u> <u>programme</u> this <u>summer</u> in order to get fit.
It is <u>common</u> to make a <u>summary</u> of your notes when learning for a <u>grammar</u> test.
My negative <u>comment</u> was criticised.
After many days of hiking they reached the <u>summit</u> of the mountain.
I am going to lie in the <u>hammock</u> and read my book.

d. Various answers are possible, for example:
Will the judge summon me to court if I don't pay the fine?
I tried to summon up the courage to tell my parents I had lied to them.

I enjoyed the beautiful view from the summit of the mountain.
The environmentalists met at a summit to discuss ways to protect our environment.

The gimmick caught my attention as I had never seen anything like it.
Don't be fooled. That is just a sales gimmick, not a genuine offer.

High-rise buildings are a common sight in cities.
It is common courtesy to say thank you when you receive a gift.

I watched an interesting programme on television last night.
Take this programme of events home to your parents so they know when and where everything is happening during our open day.

Exercise 7 Page 104

a. announce
annoying
antenna (or ant)
banner
beginning
bunny
cannibal
can not
centennial (or cent)
channel
cinnamon
connect
cunning
dinner (or in / inn / inner)
funnel
innocent (or cent)
mannequin
meanness (or an)
pennant
questionnaire
son net (or on)
tunnel
tyranny
unnecessary

b. antenna   →   thin sensory organs found in pairs on some heads
cannibal   →   someone who eats people
cinnamon   →   a spice from the bark of a tree

channel	→	a strip of water between land
centennial	→	relating to a hundred years
tunnel	→	a passage through something
mannequin	→	a life-size dummy on which clothes are displayed
pennant	→	a small triangular flag on ships so they can be identified
sonnet	→	a poem with 14 lines and a set structure
tyranny	→	cruel use of power over people

c. annoying, cunning, innocent, unnecessary

d.
beginning	→	ending
connect	→	disconnect
cannot	→	can
innocent	→	guilty
meanness	→	kindness
unnecessary	→	necessary

e. Any sentences using the given words, for example:
I have to announce the notices at our school assembly.
The ship's funnel blew a loud farewell to the harbour.
The dinner that we ate at the hotel to celebrate my grandparents' wedding anniversary was delicious.
To file my tax return I had to complete a long questionnaire.
I see numerous bunny rabbits in the field on my morning run.

Exercise 8 Pages 105–106

a.
ar • range • ment	con • fer • ring	nar • row	sor • ry
ar • ray	cor • re • spond	oc • cur • ring	straw • ber • ry
ar • rest	cur • rent	oc • cur • rence	sur • ren • der
bar • rel	em • bar • rassed	par • rot	sur • round
bar • rier	er • rand	pre • fer • ring	ter • rain
car • riage	hor • ror	quar • rel	ter • ri • ble
car • rot	ir • reg • u • lar	quar • ry	to • mor • row
car • ry	mir • ror	re • fer • ring	wor • ry

The syllables are divided between the two 'r's in rr words.

b.
arrest	→	capture
carry	→	transport
conferred	→	discussed
correspond	→	match
errand	→	task

53

embarrassed   →   ashamed
preferred   →   favoured
referred   →   mentioned
surround   →   enclose
surrender   →   submit

c. narrow   →   wide
    irregular   →   regular
    terrible   →   wonderful
    sorry   →   glad
    worry   →   reassure

d. arrange, occur, regular, confer, embarrass, prefer

e. happening   →   occurring
    an orange root vegetable   →   carrot
    a container in the shape of a cylinder   →   barrel
    water or air moving in one direction   →   current
    talking bird   →   parrot
    a stretch of land   →   terrain
    an area where stone is mined   →   quarry
    reflecting glass   →   mirror
    a form of transport drawn by a horse   →   carriage
    great fear and dislike   →   horror
    an angry disagreement   →   quarrel
    the next day   →   tomorrow

Exercise 9   Page 107

a. messenger – takes messages
missionary – takes their religion to another country

b.

Verb	+ ed	+ ing
assemble	assembled	assembling
assign	assigned	assigning
assist	assisted	assisting
assume	assumed	assuming
assure	assured	assuring

Verb	+ ed	+ ing
harass	harassed	harassing
process	processed	processing
massage	massaged	massaging

c. grasshopper
   pressure
   permission
   essay
   wireless
   necessity
   discussion
   expression

d. I can <u>assure</u> you that it is <u>necessary</u> to look right and left before you walk <u>across</u> the road.
   Keep your mobile phone in your <u>possession</u> at all times <u>unless</u> you want it to disappear.
   The Olympics will <u>assemble</u> talented athletes from many places around the world.
   <u>Admission</u> to the club is reserved for <u>business</u> people.
   I love eating the boxes of <u>assorted</u> biscuits.

Exercise 10 Pages 108–109

a. attention, committee, written, attitude, cattle, kitten, rattle, flatten, bottom, bottle

b.
an insect with two pairs of wings	→	butterfly
used to boil water	→	kettle
a small house	→	cottage
a baby's toy	→	rattle
a type of material	→	cotton
string-shaped pasta	→	spaghetti
to refuse to have anything to do with something	→	boycott
having an attractive face	→	pretty
a repetitive design	→	pattern
something that appears dark, but is surrounded by light	→	silhouette

c. Any sentences using forms of the sets of words given, for example:
   1. The pretty butterfly fluttered by.
   2. I am already so attached to my new little kittens.
   3. The oil painting depicted a sea regatta in silhouette using a palette of pastel colours.

d.

B	U	T	T	O	N	Z	S	M	W	
S	S	M	P	O	M	A	C	N	I	
A	T	T	A	C	H	T	A	R	K	
T	S	M	P	U	L	T	T	E	P	
T	E	B	T	A	I	E	T	G	A	
R	T	E	R	K	T	M	E	A	L	
A	T	O	Z	K	T	P	R	T	E	
C	L	U	Q	D	L	T	H	T	T	
T	E	N	L	G	E	N	Y	A	T	
D	A	T	T	I	C	G	Q	P	E	

e. a fruit: a<u>pp</u>le
use violence to harm: a<u>tt</u>ack
you wear pumps in this dance: ba<u>ll</u>et
you blow these up for parties: ba<u>ll</u>oons
something soldiers do: ba<u>tt</u>le
another word for stomach: be<u>ll</u>y
you can blow these: bu<u>bb</u>les
this could kill you: bu<u>ll</u>et
cows munch this: gra<u>ss</u>
not sad: ha<u>pp</u>y
a pastime: ho<u>bb</u>y
opposite of nice: ho<u>rr</u>ible

this boils water: ke<u>tt</u>le
this involves lips: ki<u>ss</u>
a baby cat: ki<u>tt</u>en
the partner of salt: pe<u>pp</u>er
a sweet dessert: pu<u>dd</u>ing
this will wet your shoes: pu<u>dd</u>le
a jigsaw: pu<u>zz</u>le
a type of puzzle: ri<u>dd</u>le
this causes sliding: sli<u>pp</u>ery
what this book is about: spe<u>ll</u>ing
a clear, hot day: su<u>nn</u>y
not the loser: wi<u>nn</u>er

Using the apostrophe correctly

Exercise 1 Page 111

a. we are, was not, cannot, do not, did not, it is, you are, I am, he is or he has, we will, they have, will not

b. It's
You've
doesn't
We'll
She'd
They're
I'd
It's not/It isn't, you're

c. Any sentences that demonstrate the difference in meaning of the given words with and without the apostrophe, for example:
  1. <u>He'll</u> be here in a minute.
    It was <u>hell</u> working in the uncomfortable conditions.
  2. <u>She'll</u> break her leg climbing on that high wall.
    I love collecting <u>shells</u> from the beach to make a pretty display.
  3. <u>I'll</u> never forget what you've done for me.
    After standing in the freezing rain for two hours watching the football match,
    I fell <u>ill</u>.
  4. <u>We'll</u> win the dance competition if we keep practising.
    In less developed countries people draw their water from a <u>well</u>.
  5. "<u>We're</u> winning," shouted the small boy excitedly.
    "We <u>were</u> winning, but now we've lost," he said with disappointment.
  6. <u>They're</u> going to be late if they keep dawdling like that.
    <u>There</u>'s a new ice cream parlour in the park.
  7. <u>She'd</u> better have a good excuse.
    We keep our garden tools in the <u>shed</u>.

Exercise 2 Pages 112–114

a. the teacher's class
the car's engine
the cat's whiskers
the boy's sister
the father's coat
my brother's school
my friend's parents

the dog's collar
John and Simon's bedroom
Anne and Peter's house
Tom, Dick and Harry's adventures
the children's games
the team's work
the men's houses
the pupils' desks
the books' titles
the elephants' trunks
the birds' cages
the kittens' cries
the boys' mothers
the actors' costumes
the navies' ships

b. The <u>ship's</u> captain has his own table.
I used my <u>mother's</u> phone.
<u>John and Cathy's</u> garden is untidy.
Nia is waiting at the <u>nurse's</u> office.
The <u>baby's</u> shoes are under the bed.
The <u>postmen's</u> bags are always heavy.
The <u>city's</u> air is polluted.
The <u>ladies'</u> committee sold tickets for the raffle.
The <u>players'</u> bags are in locker room.
The inspector checked all the <u>passengers'</u> tickets.
The <u>girls'</u> mothers are outside.
The dog wagged <u>its</u> tail.
Those shoes are <u>hers</u>.

c. The neck belongs to the giraffe.
The feet belong to the giraffes.
The whiskers belong to the cat.
The paws belong to the cats.
The books belong to the boys.
The pencil belongs to the boy.
The staffroom belongs to the teachers.
The office belongs to the principal and vice-principal.
The eggs belong to the birds.

Extend your vocabulary
Exercise 1 Pages 115–116

a. Any synonyms for the given words, for example:

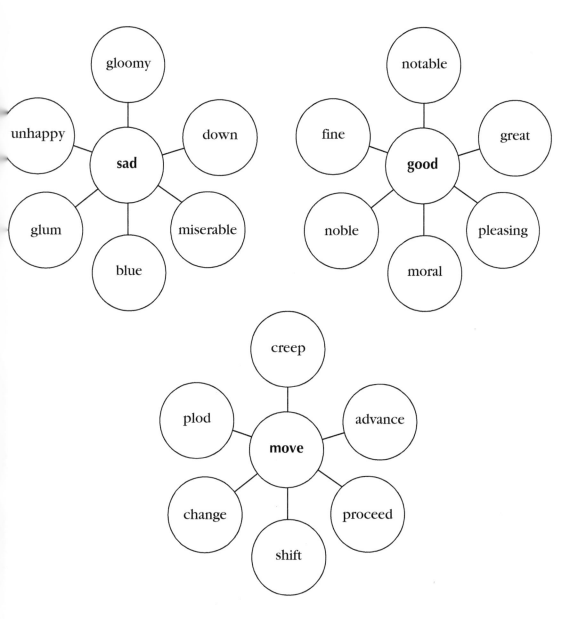

b. The unkind children <u>teased</u> the girl when she made a mistake.
I cannot concentrate as I feel <u>lazy</u>.
I will not have more as I have had <u>enough</u>.
My mother <u>forced</u> me to attend.
The racing car travelled at great <u>speed</u>.

c. show, thin, happy, sad, need

d. **1.** ingenious
   2. heartened
   3. conclude
   4. sad
   5. scrawny

e. I <u>gazed</u> longingly at the beautiful day and wished I wasn't stuck inside working.
We <u>watched</u> television last night.
He was an eye-witness as he <u>observed</u> the accident happen.
Have you <u>noticed</u> how much alike they are?
They <u>looked</u> at the pictures for ages, but could not find one difference between them.
She <u>stared</u> at the cut on her leg.

f. and, try, end, old, big, ask, dig, mad,
wet, sad, fat, buy, top, cry

Exercise 2 Pages 117–118

a. in   →   out
    give   →   take
    come   →   go
    up   →   down
    buy   →   sell
    dead   →   alive
    life   →   death
    off   →   on
Any sentences that use the pairs, for example:
Every time customers came <u>in</u> or went <u>out</u>, a cold draught blew through the shop.
If I <u>give</u> you my book please will you <u>take</u> it to the teacher.
If you <u>come</u> to my house after school we can <u>go</u> to cricket practice together.
The hot-air balloon rose <u>up</u> into the sky before coming <u>down</u> gently an hour later.
I <u>buy</u> vegetables from a farmer and <u>sell</u> them to customers at the market.
'Wanted – <u>dead</u> or <u>alive</u>' stated the Wild West poster.
"This is a matter of <u>life</u> or <u>death</u>," shouted the policeman as he ran through the town centre.
Energy-saving experts advise you to switch <u>off</u> the light switch when you're not using it and only turn it <u>on</u> when you need it.

b. Any appropriate antonyms, for example:
I am going to <u>subtract</u> these numbers to get the answer.
The accused was found <u>innocent</u>.
We swam in very <u>warm</u> <u>murky</u> water.
I am allowed to buy <u>cheap</u> presents.
I <u>seldom</u> visit my grandmother in hospital.

c. Any antonyms for the given words, for example:

awesome	→	awful
big	→	small
colourful	→	drab
daring	→	cowardly
exciting	→	boring
fat	→	thin
glad	→	sad
hot	→	cold
inside	→	outside
join	→	leave
kind	→	unkind
loyal	→	disloyal
majority	→	minority
neat	→	messy
open	→	closed
plural	→	singular
quiet	→	noisy
rise	→	fall
same	→	different
tall	→	short
used	→	disused
vain	→	modest
weak	→	strong
exhale	→	inhale
young	→	old
zealous	→	unenthusiastic

d. anticlockwise, irregular, improper, incomplete, illegal

e. hopeless, thoughtful, helpless, harmful, useless

Exercise 3 Pages 119–121

a.

ball	→	bawl
bald	→	balled
bare	→	bear
die	→	dye
draft	→	draught
find	→	fined
flu	→	flew
flour	→	flower
fur	→	fir
graft	→	graphed
heel	→	heal
here	→	hear
male	→	mail
meet	→	meat
piece	→	peace
rain	→	reign
write	→	right
rode	→	road
stare	→	stair
through	→	threw
week	→	weak

b. He sat <u>by</u> the fire.
She <u>prayed</u> for <u>peace</u>.
Last <u>week</u> I had the <u>flu</u>.
I <u>rode</u> my bike to the <u>beach</u>.
<u>Which</u> book is yours?

c. We are not <u>allowed</u> to talk in class.
In English lessons we have to read <u>aloud</u>.
My bicycle hasn't got any <u>brakes</u> so I can't stop very quickly.
My sister is very clumsy, she often <u>breaks</u> things.
I'm tired of lending you money. I'm not giving you another <u>cent</u>.
Those flowers have a very strong <u>scent</u>.
We saw a large <u>herd</u> of buffalo in the game reserve.
I <u>heard</u> my favourite song on the radio.
The boy threw a stone and cracked the window <u>pane</u>.
He went to the doctor because he had a <u>pain</u> in his chest.
We are going to the airport to catch a <u>plane</u> to London.
The animals roamed across the <u>plain</u>.
I'm going to school. Are you coming <u>too</u>?
We will be home at <u>two</u> o'clock.

d. Various answers are possible, for example:

1. Whether the weather is warm or whether it's cold, we'll be going to the beach on the weekend.
2. The principal dancer believed in the principle of 'bad dress rehearsal, good live performance'.
3. In the past week I have passed the house with the ugly dog seven times.
4. I am bored with staring at this chess board waiting for you to make your move.
5. On my English course I was taught not to use coarse language.
6. The train fare is a fair price for that journey.

e. The medals were made of 9 <u>carat</u> gold.

The fishermen picked <u>mussels</u> from the rocks.

When you collect data you have to find a suitable <u>source</u>.

After the bride walked down the <u>aisle</u>, the <u>bridal</u> party went to the park to have photos taken.

My sister and I like to <u>wander</u> around the mall.

Put your bags down over <u>there</u>.

Exercise 4 Page 121

Various second meanings could be added to the table, for example:

Homonym	Meaning 1	Meaning 2
ball	formal dance	spherical object used for sport
bat	flying rodent	wooden object for hitting ball
cricket	insect	sport in which you score runs
cold	illness	at a low temperature
date	fruit from a palm tree	the day, month and year
fair	just, treating everyone the same	neither good nor bad
glasses	drinking containers	spectacles
jam	fruit spread for bread	lots of traffic
record	write down	best accomplishment
second	unit of time	after first
spring	coiled metal object	season before summer
tip	money given to a waiter	pour
trip	fall over something	journey

Exercise 5 Pages 122–123

a. Oral exercise

b.

bass	type of fish	musical instrument	a deep sound
bow	lean down	weapon used with an arrow	ribbon
close	nearby	shut	almost
conduct	behaviour	lead an orchestra	
content		satisfied	information inside a book
desert	leave behind	dry, sandy region	
does	female deer	present tense of do	
invalid	not true		a sick person

c. Various answers are possible, for example:
Lead is used to make pencils.
I live in London.
Tadpoles are so small you could describe them as minute.
The museum contains many interesting objects.
I am going to perfect my speech by reading it over and over.
Pierogi is a popular Polish food.
My favourite Christmas present was a book of poetry.
I read my poetry book on Christmas night.

d. row
sow
second
record
project

e. tear
wind
wound
use
subject

Exercise 6 Pages 124–125

a. My mother and aunt met me at the airport. My sister wasn't with them because she was at school. My father was visiting my grandfather in hospital. I feel sorry for him. He is very sick.

b. | Masculine | Feminine |
|---|---|
| prince | daughter |
| waiter | duchess |
| bridegroom | actress |
| host | mayoress |
| widower | congresswoman |
| congressman | princess |
| actor | bride |
| son | widow |
| mayor | hostess |
| duke | waitress |

c. Any pairs of names for male / female professionals, for example:
policeman – policewoman
headmaster – headmistress
waiter – waitress
air steward – air stewardess
author – authoress
conductor – conductress
manager – manageress
poet – poetess

d. Any names for professionals of either gender, for example:
accountant, architect, dentist, doctor, editor, engineer, interpreter, journalist,
lawyer, optician, nurse, pharmacist, pilot, professor, psychologist, surgeon, teacher,
translator, vet

e. brother-in-law
bachelor
queen
cousin
aunt

Exercise 7 Page 126

stallion	→	mare
ram	→	ewe
gander	→	goose
bull	→	cow
boar	→	sow
colt	→	filly
fox	→	vixen
drake	→	duck
buck	→	doe

Exercise 8 Page 127

a. A young fox is a <u>cub</u>.
A young fish is a <u>fry</u>.
An adult calf is a <u>cow</u>, <u>bull</u>, <u>elephant</u> or a <u>whale</u>.
A young eel is an <u>elver</u>.
A young owl is an <u>owlet</u>.
A young frog is a <u>tadpole</u>.
An adult parr is a <u>salmon</u>.
An adult joey is a <u>kangaroo</u>.
A young goat is a <u>kid</u>.
A young butterfly or moth is a <u>caterpillar</u>.

b.

bear	→	cub
deer	→	fawn
bird	→	nestling
eagle	→	eaglet
lion	→	cub
sheep	→	lamb
swan	→	cygnet
goose	→	gosling
horse	→	foal
hen	→	chicken
pig	→	piglet
duck	→	duckling
cat	→	kitten
dog	→	puppy

Exercise 9 Pages 128–129

a. An elephant <u>trumpets</u>.
A donkey <u>brays</u>.
A <u>goose</u> cackles and hisses.
A monkey <u>chatters</u>.
An <u>eagle</u> screams.
A pig <u>grunts</u>.
An <u>ape</u> gibbers.
A snake <u>hisses</u>.
A <u>wolf</u> howls.
A frog <u>croaks</u>.

b. Any examples of animal / sound alliteration, for example:
  Bees buzz busily
  Bulls bellow brazenly
  Crows caw callously
  Crickets chirp cheerily

c.

Masculine	Feminine	Diminutive	Sound
bull	cow	calf	low
boar	sow	piglet	grunt
lion	lioness	cub	roar
bull-elephant	cow-elephant	calf	trumpet
billy-goat	nanny-goat	kid	bleat
stallion	mare	foal	neigh

d.

chickens	→	peep
doves	→	coo
hyenas	→	laugh
turkeys	→	gobble
bears	→	growl
beetles	→	drone
ducks	→	quack
cows	→	low
hens	→	cackle
owls	→	hoot
snakes	→	hiss
wolves	→	howl

First aid for common spelling problems
Exercise 1 Pages 132–133

a. threw
stationery
right
pear
steel
passed
site

b. He walked <u>past</u> the window.
The traffic was <u>stationary</u> because of an accident.
<u>They're</u> waiting for a bus.
Only <u>two</u> students were late for class.
Please <u>accept</u> my apologies for being late.
The teacher sent the late-comers to the <u>principal</u>.
I hate it when I <u>lose</u> my pencil.
She has <u>a lot</u> of shoes.

c. Various answers are possible, for example:
1. We <u>rein</u> in the horses in the <u>rain</u>.
2. At the boat show, there was a <u>sale</u> of <u>sails</u>.
3. <u>Oars</u> cannot be made of iron <u>ore</u> as it is too heavy.
4. <u>Mites</u> <u>might</u> infest your bed.
5. The church on the <u>isle</u> had an <u>aisle</u> decorated with beautiful flowers.
6. When learning to read, children are <u>allowed</u> to read <u>aloud</u>.
7. A <u>larva</u> cannot survive in <u>lava</u>.
8. The children became <u>bored</u> waiting for the teacher to write on the <u>board</u>.
9. I want to lose weight from my <u>waist</u> but I don't want to <u>waste</u> my food.

d. She cut her foot on a <u>piece</u> of glass.
I read the <u>whole</u> book last week.
An eagle is a bird of <u>prey</u>.
She felt sick, so she went to <u>lie</u> down.
My eyes are as heavy as <u>lead</u>.
It's <u>already</u> four o'clock.
We are going to have ice cream for <u>dessert</u>.
Be careful or you will <u>break</u> something.

Exercise 2 Pages 134–135

a. Methods explained in question book on pages 2-10.

b. 1. accommodation
    2. bicycle
    3. continuous
    4. definitely
    5. desperate
    6. embarrass
    7. forehead
    8. length
    9. occasion
    10. parallel
    11. separate
    12. tomorrow
    13. yacht

c. We took our sick dog to the <u>veterinary</u> clinic.
   We received a two year <u>guarantee</u> when we bought a new television.
   The technician came and put up a special <u>aerial</u> on the roof so we could get good television reception.
   That store gives good service. I would highly <u>recommend</u> them.
   I'll have to check the <u>calendar</u> to see what day of the week that is.
   It was not so big! Don't <u>exaggerate</u>.
   We had to stand in a <u>queue</u> for a very long time before we were served.
   I <u>sincerely</u> hope that he gets better soon.

d. Any wordsearch including ten words from the list

e. Students to work together

Useful words to know

Exercise 1 Page 137

a.

minute	→	sixty seconds
dawn	→	first light of the day as the sun rises
day	→	twenty-four hours
dusk	→	just before the sky becomes dark at night
decade	→	ten years
hour	→	sixty minutes
millennium	→	a thousand years
p.m.	→	after noon
a.m.	→	before noon
century	→	a hundred years
year	→	365 days
leap year	→	366 days

b. Thirty days hath <u>September</u>,
April, June, and <u>November</u>;
All the rest have <u>thirty-one</u>,
Save <u>February</u>, with twenty-eight days clear,
And twenty-nine each <u>leap</u> year.

c. Any activities done on the four days of the week given, for example:
Sunday: <u>I go to church</u>.
Monday: <u>I go to Brownies</u>.
Friday: <u>I go swimming</u>.
Saturday: <u>I play football</u>.

d. <u>Yesterday</u> I spent all <u>day</u> learning for a vocabulary test. In 2030 <u>AD</u> I do not plan to work from <u>Monday</u> to <u>Friday</u>. I want to be able to fish from <u>dawn</u> to <u>dusk</u>. I will wake at 5 <u>a.m.</u> to watch the <u>sunrise</u> and make every <u>second</u> of every <u>minute</u> count.

Exercise 2 Pages 138–139

a. Three from each of the columns:

Measurement of length	Measurement of weight	Measurement of volume
millimetre	milligram	millilitre
centimetre	centigram	centilitre
decimetre	decigram	decilitre
metre	gram	litre
hectometre	hectogram	hectolitre
kilometre	kilogram	kilolitre
inch	ounce	pint
foot	pound	quart
yard		gallon

b. A <u>dozen</u> is a group of twelve.
   A <u>foot</u> is equal to 30.48 cm or 12 in.
   A <u>pound</u> is equal to 16 oz and 0.45 kg.
   A <u>centimetre</u> is equal to 10 mm.
   A <u>kilogram</u> is equal to 1000 g.
   A <u>metre</u> is equal to 100 cm.
   A <u>decimetre</u> is equal to 1/10 of a metre.
   A <u>hectogram</u> is equal to 100 grams.

c. millimetre   millilitre
   centimetre   kilometre
   decigram   hectometre
   hectogram   milligram
   kilolitre   litre

Exercise 3 Pages 139–140

a. Any description on one of the given topics that uses onomatopoeic words from the list, for example:
An accident:
The train <u>whistled</u> and <u>creaked</u> as it <u>zoomed</u> along the old rails until there was a loud <u>crash</u> as it <u>clattered</u> through the fence and <u>roared</u> down the hill, coming to a stop with a <u>thump</u>.

b. The <u>roaring</u> wind <u>howled</u> through the trees making the leaves <u>rustle</u>.
With a loud <u>clatter</u> and a <u>crash</u>, the dishes landed on the floor.
The oil <u>splattered</u> all over the stove as the bacon <u>sizzled</u> away.
The boy <u>whistled</u> as he saw a snake <u>slither</u> between the <u>fluttering</u> washing.
There was a <u>thud</u> on the stairs and then the door <u>creaked</u> open.

c. Any words suitable for describing waves in the sea or a storm, for example:
Waves in the sea: blue, choppy, crashing, rolling, swelling
A storm: bright, crashing, loud, whipping, windy

Exercise 4 Pages 140–141

a. Oral exercise

b. 'I did steal the money,' <u>confessed</u> the criminal.
'That is the funniest story I have ever heard,' <u>laughed</u> Dad.
'And you expect me to believe that tall tale,' <u>sniggered</u> Mum.
'I'm in agony,' <u>moaned</u> my sister.
'It's alive!' <u>shrieked</u> my cousin as she sprang on the table.
'I did not do it,' <u>denied</u> my brother.
'You had better be careful or I'll show you whose boss later,' <u>snarled</u> the bully.
'You will write a science test on Wednesday,' <u>announced</u> my teacher.
'You have to take this one,' <u>insisted</u> my friend.
'I think you are right,' <u>agreed</u> my grandmother.

c. mumble
exclaim
protest
chuckle
sob

d. 'If you want to be prepared for the test, you need to learn how to spell the words,' <u>advised</u> my mother.
'I do not want to go,' <u>protested</u> my nephew.
'That is how it is going to be from now on,' <u>declared</u> my grandfather.
'I suppose I should start studying,' <u>admitted</u> my niece.

Exercise 5 Page 142

a. amble → to move slowly and reluctantly
bob → to bounce up and down frequently especially in water
bounce → to jump up and down
bustle → to hurry around getting things organised
crawl → to move on your hands and knees
creep → to move very quietly
dawdle → to walk in a slow relaxed way
drift → to move aimlessly in an unforced, unhurried way
droop → to move in a dejected way with your head and body sagging limply
frolic → to move in a lively and carefree way

b. limp → hobble
slump → slouch
fly → soar
jump → pounce
float → glide
shove → jostle
spin → whirl
squirm → wriggle
stumble → stagger

c. Drama exercise

d. Definitions should be similar to the following:
loiter – to move slowly, stopping often
lope – to run using long steps
lurch – to move while making sudden movements
plod – to walk as if with heavy feet
plunge – to move suddenly and often a long way down

Exercise 6 Pages 143–144

a. azure
cobalt
indigo
navy
sapphire
turquoise

b. auburn
carmine
crimson
magenta
scarlet

c. Examples of any ten colour shades from the word list with their names

d. Any sets of five colours that match the table headings, for example:

Brilliant (bright, vivid) colours	Drab (dull, dowdy) colours	Gaudy (flashy, showy) colours
yellow	brown	gold
cobalt	grey	silver
fuchsia	beige	scarlet
emerald	khaki	crimson
red	mustard	purple

e. Various answers are possible, for example:
1. Shades of white
2. Shades of green
3. Shades of purple
4. Metallic shades
5. Earthy shades

f. Anything students may associate with the given colours, for example:
white – cleanliness, purity, snow
black – fear, grief, night
grey – drabness, storm clouds, uncertainty
blue – boys, sea, sky
green – calm, envy, grass
yellow – happiness, jealousy, sun
purple – power, religion, sophistication
orange – excitement, joy, sun

g. Any comparisons with something of similar colour, for example:

As white as a landscape of snow.

As black as the moonless night.

As pink as a Valentine's heart.

As purple as a field of crocuses.

As yellow as the sun in a bright blue sky.

As gold as the Queen's crown.

As silver as my grandparents' hair.

As turquoise as the Caribbean sea.